40 Bacon Recipes for Home

By: Kelly Johnson

Table of Contents

Breakfast and Brunch:

- Classic Bacon and Eggs
- Bacon and Cheddar Breakfast Casserole
- Bacon Pancakes with Maple Syrup
- Bacon and Cheese Stuffed French Toast
- Bacon, Egg, and Cheese Breakfast Burrito
- Bacon and Spinach Quiche
- Bacon and Hash Brown Breakfast Skillet
- Bacon and Avocado Breakfast Sandwich
- Bacon and Cheese Breakfast Quesadilla
- Bacon and Potato Breakfast Tacos

Appetizers and Snacks:

- Bacon-Wrapped Jalapeño Poppers
- Bacon-Wrapped Water Chestnuts
- Bacon-Wrapped Dates with Goat Cheese
- Bacon and Cheddar Stuffed Mushrooms
- Bacon-Wrapped Asparagus
- Candied Bacon Bites
- Bacon-Wrapped Shrimp Skewers
- Bacon and Cheese Stuffed Jalapeño
- Bacon-Wrapped Potato Bites
- Bacon-Wrapped Mozzarella Sticks

Main Courses:

- Bacon-Wrapped Meatloaf
- Bacon-Wrapped Chicken Breast
- Bacon-Wrapped Pork Tenderloin
- Bacon-Wrapped BBQ Chicken Skewers
- Bacon and Mushroom Stuffed Chicken Thighs
- Bacon-Wrapped Salmon
  Bacon and Cheese Stuffed Burgers
- Bacon-Wrapped BBQ Meatballs
- Bacon-Wrapped Filet Mignon

- Bacon-Wrapped BBQ Shrimp

Salads and Sides:

- Bacon and Blue Cheese Wedge Salad
- Bacon and Brussels Sprouts Salad
- Loaded Baked Potato Salad with Bacon
- Bacon-Wrapped Asparagus Bundles
- Bacon and Corn Salad
- Creamy Bacon Coleslaw
- Bacon and Cheese Loaded Sweet Potatoes
- Bacon and Ranch Pasta Salad
- Bacon and Garlic Green Beans
- Bacon and Potato Casserole

Breakfast and Brunch:

Classic Bacon and Eggs

Ingredients:

- 4 slices of bacon
- 4 large eggs
- Salt and pepper to taste
- Chopped fresh chives or parsley for garnish (optional)

Instructions:

- Cook Bacon:
  - In a large skillet over medium heat, cook the bacon until it reaches your desired level of crispiness. Remove the bacon from the skillet and place it on a paper towel-lined plate to drain excess grease.
- Prepare Eggs:
  - Depending on your preference, you can fry, scramble, or poach the eggs. Here's a simple way to fry them:
    - In the same skillet with the bacon grease, crack the eggs into the pan. Cook them to your liking—over easy, medium, or well-done.
- Season and Serve:
  - Season the eggs with salt and pepper to taste. Sprinkle with chopped chives or parsley if desired.
- Serve:
  - Plate the eggs alongside the crispy bacon. Enjoy your classic bacon and eggs breakfast!

Tip: For added variety, consider serving the eggs on toast, as a breakfast sandwich, or alongside sautéed vegetables.

Feel free to modify the recipe based on your preferences and add any additional elements you enjoy!

Bacon and Cheddar Breakfast Casserole

Ingredients:

- 8 slices of bacon, cooked and crumbled
- 8 large eggs
- 2 cups shredded cheddar cheese
- 2 cups milk
- 1 teaspoon Dijon mustard
- 1 teaspoon salt
- 1/2 teaspoon black pepper
- 1/2 teaspoon garlic powder
- 1/2 teaspoon onion powder
- 6 cups cubed bread (such as French bread or ciabatta), slightly stale for better absorption
- 1/4 cup green onions, finely chopped (optional, for garnish)

Instructions:

Preheat Oven:
- Preheat your oven to 350°F (175°C). Grease a 9x13-inch baking dish.

Prepare Bacon:
- Cook the bacon until crispy, then crumble it into small pieces.

Prepare Bread Cubes:
- Cut the bread into bite-sized cubes.

Whisk Egg Mixture:
- In a large mixing bowl, whisk together the eggs, milk, Dijon mustard, salt, pepper, garlic powder, and onion powder until well combined.

Assemble Casserole:
- Place half of the bread cubes into the prepared baking dish. Sprinkle half of the crumbled bacon and shredded cheddar cheese over the bread. Repeat the layers with the remaining bread, bacon, and cheese.

Pour Egg Mixture:
- Pour the egg mixture evenly over the layered ingredients, ensuring that the bread is well-soaked.

Allow to Soak:
- Allow the casserole to sit for about 15 minutes, giving the bread time to absorb the egg mixture.

Bake:
- Bake in the preheated oven for 40-45 minutes or until the top is golden brown, and the center is set.

Garnish and Serve:
- If desired, garnish with chopped green onions. Let it cool for a few minutes before slicing and serving.

This Bacon and Cheddar Breakfast Casserole is perfect for feeding a crowd during brunch or making ahead for busy mornings. Enjoy!

Bacon Pancakes with Maple Syrup

Ingredients:

- 1 cup all-purpose flour
- 2 tablespoons granulated sugar
- 1 teaspoon baking powder
- 1/2 teaspoon baking soda
- 1/4 teaspoon salt
- 1 cup buttermilk
- 1 large egg
- 2 tablespoons unsalted butter, melted
- 4 slices of bacon, cooked and crumbled
- Maple syrup for serving

Instructions:

Prepare Bacon:
- Cook the bacon until crispy, then crumble it into small pieces. Set aside.

Preheat Griddle or Pan:
- Preheat a griddle or non-stick pan over medium heat.

Prepare Dry Ingredients:
- In a large bowl, whisk together the flour, sugar, baking powder, baking soda, and salt.

Prepare Wet Ingredients:
- In another bowl, whisk together the buttermilk, egg, and melted butter.

Combine Wet and Dry Ingredients:
- Pour the wet ingredients into the dry ingredients and stir until just combined. Do not overmix; a few lumps are okay.

Add Bacon:
- Gently fold in the crumbled bacon into the pancake batter.

Cook Pancakes:
- Ladle the batter onto the preheated griddle, using about 1/4 cup for each pancake. Cook until bubbles form on the surface, then flip and cook the other side until golden brown.

Serve:
- Serve the bacon pancakes warm, drizzled with maple syrup.

Optional Garnish:
- Consider adding additional crumbled bacon on top or a dollop of whipped cream for extra indulgence.

Enjoy these delicious Bacon Pancakes with Maple Syrup for a sweet and savory breakfast treat!

Bacon and Cheese Stuffed French Toast

Ingredients:

For the Filling:

- 8 slices of bacon, cooked and crumbled
- 1 cup shredded cheddar cheese

For the French Toast:

- 8 slices of thick-cut bread (such as brioche or challah)
- 4 large eggs
- 1 cup milk
- 1 teaspoon vanilla extract
- 1/2 teaspoon ground cinnamon
- Pinch of salt

For Cooking:

- Butter for cooking
- Maple syrup for serving

Instructions:

Prepare Bacon and Cheese Filling:
- In a bowl, mix the crumbled bacon and shredded cheddar cheese until well combined. Set aside.

Make the French Toast Batter:
- In a shallow dish, whisk together eggs, milk, vanilla extract, ground cinnamon, and a pinch of salt.

Assemble Stuffed French Toast:
- Lay out 4 slices of bread and evenly distribute the bacon and cheese filling on top, spreading it to the edges. Top each with another slice of bread to create sandwiches.

Soak in Egg Mixture:
- Dip each stuffed sandwich into the egg mixture, ensuring both sides are well-coated. Allow excess batter to drip off.

Cook French Toast:
- In a skillet or griddle over medium heat, melt butter. Cook each stuffed French toast sandwich until golden brown on both sides and the cheese is melted inside.

Serve:
- Remove from the pan and let them rest for a minute. Cut each sandwich in half diagonally and serve hot.

Optional Garnish:
- Drizzle with maple syrup and sprinkle a little extra bacon on top for a finishing touch.

Enjoy the delightful combination of sweet and savory with this Bacon and Cheese Stuffed French Toast!

Bacon, Egg, and Cheese Breakfast Burrito

Ingredients:

- 4 large flour tortillas
- 8 slices of bacon, cooked and crumbled
- 4 large eggs
- Salt and pepper to taste
- 1 cup shredded cheddar cheese
- 1 tablespoon butter
- Salsa or hot sauce for serving (optional)
- Chopped fresh cilantro or green onions for garnish (optional)

Instructions:

Cook Bacon:
- In a skillet over medium heat, cook the bacon until crispy. Remove from the skillet, drain excess grease, and crumble it. Set aside.

Prepare Eggs:
- In the same skillet, melt butter. Crack the eggs into the skillet, season with salt and pepper, and scramble until cooked to your liking.

Assemble Burritos:
- Warm the tortillas in the microwave or on a griddle. Lay out each tortilla, and in the center, distribute the scrambled eggs, crumbled bacon, and shredded cheddar cheese.

Fold and Roll:
- Fold in the sides of the tortilla and then roll it up from the bottom to create a burrito.

Serve:
- Place the burritos seam-side down on a plate. If desired, top with salsa or hot sauce for an extra kick.

Optional Garnish:
- Garnish with chopped cilantro or green onions for freshness.

Serve Warm:
- Serve the Bacon, Egg, and Cheese Breakfast Burritos warm for a delicious and satisfying breakfast.

These burritos are not only quick to make but also customizable to suit your taste. Feel free to add ingredients like diced tomatoes, avocados, or sour cream for additional flavor. Enjoy!

Bacon and Spinach Quiche

Ingredients:

For the Quiche Filling:

- 1 pie crust (store-bought or homemade)
- 8 slices of bacon, cooked and crumbled
- 1 cup fresh spinach, chopped
- 1 cup shredded Swiss or Gruyere cheese
- 1/2 cup diced onions
- 4 large eggs
- 1 cup half-and-half or whole milk
- Salt and pepper to taste
- 1/2 teaspoon garlic powder
- 1/2 teaspoon dried thyme

Instructions:

Preheat Oven:
- Preheat your oven to 375°F (190°C).

Prepare Pie Crust:
- Roll out the pie crust and press it into a 9-inch pie dish. Crimp the edges or trim any excess.

Cook Bacon:
- In a skillet over medium heat, cook the bacon until crispy. Remove from the skillet, drain excess grease, and crumble it. Set aside.

Sauté Spinach and Onions:
- In the same skillet, sauté diced onions until translucent. Add chopped spinach and cook until wilted. Remove from heat.

Prepare Quiche Filling:
- In a bowl, whisk together eggs, half-and-half (or milk), salt, pepper, garlic powder, and dried thyme.

Assemble Quiche:
- Spread the crumbled bacon, sautéed spinach and onions, and shredded cheese evenly over the pie crust. Pour the egg mixture over the top.

Bake:
- Bake in the preheated oven for 35-40 minutes or until the quiche is set and the top is golden brown.

Cool and Slice:

- Allow the quiche to cool for a few minutes before slicing. This allows it to set further.

Serve:
- Serve slices of the Bacon and Spinach Quiche warm. It's delicious for brunch, lunch, or a light dinner.

Enjoy the rich and savory flavors of this Bacon and Spinach Quiche!

Bacon and Hash Brown Breakfast Skillet

Ingredients:

- 8 slices of bacon, chopped
- 4 cups frozen hash browns, thawed
- 1 onion, finely diced
- 1 bell pepper, diced (any color)
- 1 cup shredded cheddar cheese
- 4 large eggs
- Salt and pepper to taste
- 1 teaspoon garlic powder
- 1 teaspoon paprika
- Fresh parsley or green onions for garnish (optional)
- Hot sauce or salsa for serving (optional)

Instructions:

Cook Bacon:
- In a large oven-safe skillet over medium heat, cook the chopped bacon until crispy. Remove bacon with a slotted spoon and set aside.

Sauté Vegetables:
- In the same skillet, sauté diced onion and bell pepper until softened.

Add Hash Browns:
- Add the thawed hash browns to the skillet, spreading them evenly. Let them cook without stirring for a few minutes until the bottom gets crispy.

Season:
- Season the hash browns with salt, pepper, garlic powder, and paprika. Stir to combine.

Create Wells for Eggs:
- Make small wells in the hash browns for the eggs.

Cook Eggs:
- Crack an egg into each well. Season the eggs with salt and pepper.

Bake:
- Transfer the skillet to a preheated oven and bake at 375°F (190°C) for about 10-15 minutes, or until the eggs are cooked to your liking.

Add Cheese and Bacon:
- Sprinkle shredded cheddar cheese and the cooked bacon over the hash browns during the last few minutes of baking, allowing the cheese to melt.

Garnish and Serve:

- Allow the quiche to cool for a few minutes before slicing. This allows it to set further.

Serve:
- Serve slices of the Bacon and Spinach Quiche warm. It's delicious for brunch, lunch, or a light dinner.

Enjoy the rich and savory flavors of this Bacon and Spinach Quiche!

Bacon and Hash Brown Breakfast Skillet

Ingredients:

- 8 slices of bacon, chopped
- 4 cups frozen hash browns, thawed
- 1 onion, finely diced
- 1 bell pepper, diced (any color)
- 1 cup shredded cheddar cheese
- 4 large eggs
- Salt and pepper to taste
- 1 teaspoon garlic powder
- 1 teaspoon paprika
- Fresh parsley or green onions for garnish (optional)
- Hot sauce or salsa for serving (optional)

Instructions:

Cook Bacon:
- In a large oven-safe skillet over medium heat, cook the chopped bacon until crispy. Remove bacon with a slotted spoon and set aside.

Sauté Vegetables:
- In the same skillet, sauté diced onion and bell pepper until softened.

Add Hash Browns:
- Add the thawed hash browns to the skillet, spreading them evenly. Let them cook without stirring for a few minutes until the bottom gets crispy.

Season:
- Season the hash browns with salt, pepper, garlic powder, and paprika. Stir to combine.

Create Wells for Eggs:
- Make small wells in the hash browns for the eggs.

Cook Eggs:
- Crack an egg into each well. Season the eggs with salt and pepper.

Bake:
- Transfer the skillet to a preheated oven and bake at 375°F (190°C) for about 10-15 minutes, or until the eggs are cooked to your liking.

Add Cheese and Bacon:
- Sprinkle shredded cheddar cheese and the cooked bacon over the hash browns during the last few minutes of baking, allowing the cheese to melt.

Garnish and Serve:

- Garnish with fresh parsley or green onions if desired. Serve the Bacon and Hash Brown Breakfast Skillet hot with optional hot sauce or salsa on the side.

This hearty skillet dish is perfect for a delicious and satisfying breakfast or brunch. Enjoy!

Bacon and Avocado Breakfast Sandwich

Ingredients:

- 4 slices of bacon
- 4 eggs
- Salt and pepper to taste
- 1 ripe avocado, sliced
- 4 slices of your favorite bread (toasted if desired)
- 4 slices of cheese (cheddar, Swiss, or your preference)
- Hot sauce or sriracha (optional)

Instructions:

Cook Bacon:
- In a skillet over medium heat, cook the bacon until crispy. Remove from the skillet and drain on paper towels.

Prepare Eggs:
- In the same skillet, cook the eggs to your liking (fried, scrambled, or poached). Season with salt and pepper.

Toast Bread (Optional):
- Toast the bread slices if you prefer a crunchy texture.

Assemble Sandwich:
- On one slice of bread, place a slice of cheese, followed by the cooked bacon, avocado slices, and the cooked egg.

Add Hot Sauce (Optional):
- If you like a bit of heat, drizzle hot sauce or sriracha over the egg.

Top with Second Slice:
- Place the second slice of bread on top to create a sandwich.

Serve:
- Slice the sandwich in half diagonally and serve immediately.

Enjoy this Bacon and Avocado Breakfast Sandwich for a tasty and filling way to start your day!

Bacon and Cheese Breakfast Quesadilla

Ingredients:

- 4 large flour tortillas
- 8 slices of bacon, cooked and crumbled
- 1 cup shredded cheddar cheese
- 4 large eggs, scrambled
- 1/2 cup diced bell peppers (any color)
- 1/4 cup diced red onion
- Salt and pepper to taste
- 1 tablespoon butter or cooking oil
- Fresh cilantro or green onions for garnish (optional)
- Salsa or sour cream for serving (optional)

Instructions:

Cook Bacon:
- In a skillet over medium heat, cook the bacon until crispy. Remove from the skillet, drain on paper towels, and crumble into pieces.

Sauté Vegetables:
- In the same skillet, sauté diced bell peppers and red onion until they are softened. Remove from the skillet and set aside.

Scramble Eggs:
- In a bowl, scramble the eggs and season with salt and pepper. Cook the eggs in the skillet until just set.

Assemble Quesadillas:
- Lay out the flour tortillas. On one half of each tortilla, distribute the scrambled eggs, crumbled bacon, sautéed vegetables, and shredded cheddar cheese.

Fold and Cook:
- Fold the other half of the tortilla over the filling, creating a half-moon shape. In the same skillet, melt butter or heat oil over medium heat. Cook each quesadilla until the tortilla is crispy and the cheese is melted, about 2-3 minutes per side.

Garnish:
- If desired, garnish with fresh cilantro or green onions.

Serve:
- Slice the quesadillas into wedges and serve hot. Optional: Serve with salsa or sour cream on the side.

Enjoy this quick and delicious Bacon and Cheese Breakfast Quesadilla for a satisfying morning meal!

Bacon and Potato Breakfast Tacos

Ingredients:

For the Potato Hash:

- 2 large potatoes, peeled and diced into small cubes
- 1 small onion, finely chopped
- 2 tablespoons olive oil
- Salt and pepper to taste
- 1 teaspoon garlic powder
- 1 teaspoon paprika

For the Tacos:

- 8 small flour or corn tortillas
- 8 slices of bacon, cooked and crumbled
- 4 large eggs, scrambled
- 1 cup shredded cheddar cheese
- Salsa or hot sauce for serving
- Fresh cilantro or green onions for garnish (optional)

Instructions:

Prepare Potato Hash:
- In a skillet over medium heat, heat olive oil. Add diced potatoes and chopped onions. Season with salt, pepper, garlic powder, and paprika. Cook until the potatoes are golden brown and cooked through, stirring occasionally.

Cook Bacon and Scrambled Eggs:
- While the potatoes are cooking, prepare the bacon until crispy. Remove from the skillet, drain, and crumble. In the same skillet, cook the scrambled eggs until just set.

Assemble Tacos:
- Warm the tortillas in a dry skillet or microwave. On each tortilla, layer the potato hash, scrambled eggs, crumbled bacon, and shredded cheddar cheese.

Garnish and Serve:
- Top with fresh cilantro or green onions if desired. Serve the Bacon and Potato Breakfast Tacos with salsa or hot sauce on the side.

Optional Extras:
- Feel free to add extras like diced tomatoes, avocado slices, or a dollop of sour cream for added flavor.

Enjoy these savory and hearty Bacon and Potato Breakfast Tacos for a delicious morning treat!

Appetizers and Snacks:

Bacon-Wrapped Jalapeño Poppers

Ingredients:

- 12 large jalapeño peppers, halved lengthwise and seeds removed
- 8 ounces cream cheese, softened
- 1 cup shredded cheddar cheese
- 1 teaspoon garlic powder
- 1 teaspoon onion powder
- 12 slices of bacon, cut in half
- Toothpicks

Instructions:

Prepare Jalapeños:
- Preheat your oven to 375°F (190°C). Wear gloves while handling jalapeños to avoid irritation. Cut jalapeños in half lengthwise and remove the seeds and membranes.

Prepare Filling:
- In a bowl, mix together the softened cream cheese, shredded cheddar cheese, garlic powder, and onion powder until well combined.

Fill Jalapeños:
- Spoon the cream cheese mixture into each jalapeño half, spreading it evenly.

Wrap with Bacon:
- Wrap each stuffed jalapeño half with a half slice of bacon. Secure with toothpicks to hold the bacon in place.

Bake:
- Place the bacon-wrapped jalapeño poppers on a baking sheet lined with parchment paper. Bake in the preheated oven for 20-25 minutes or until the bacon is crispy.

Broil (Optional):
- If you want crispier bacon, you can broil the poppers for an additional 1-2 minutes, watching carefully to prevent burning.

Serve:
- Allow the bacon-wrapped jalapeño poppers to cool slightly before serving. Remove toothpicks and serve them as a delicious appetizer or party snack.

Optional Garnish:
- Garnish with chopped cilantro or green onions for added freshness.

These Bacon-Wrapped Jalapeño Poppers are a crowd-pleasing appetizer with a perfect combination of heat and creamy cheese. Enjoy responsibly!

Bacon-Wrapped Water Chestnuts

Ingredients:

- 1 can (8 ounces) whole water chestnuts, drained
- 8 slices of bacon, cut into thirds
- 1/2 cup soy sauce
- 1/2 cup brown sugar
- 1/4 cup ketchup
- 1 teaspoon minced garlic
- Toothpicks

Instructions:

Prepare Marinade:
- In a bowl, whisk together soy sauce, brown sugar, ketchup, and minced garlic to create the marinade.

Marinate Water Chestnuts:
- Place the drained water chestnuts in the marinade, ensuring they are well coated. Let them marinate for at least 30 minutes to absorb the flavors.

Preheat Oven:
- Preheat your oven to 375°F (190°C).

Wrap with Bacon:
- Take a marinated water chestnut and wrap it with a third of a bacon slice. Secure the bacon with a toothpick, piercing through the water chestnut to hold it in place.

Arrange on a Baking Sheet:
- Place the bacon-wrapped water chestnuts on a baking sheet lined with aluminum foil or parchment paper.

Bake:
- Bake in the preheated oven for 20-25 minutes or until the bacon is crispy, turning them halfway through to ensure even cooking.

Broil (Optional):
- If you prefer crispier bacon, you can broil the bacon-wrapped water chestnuts for an additional 1-2 minutes, keeping a close eye to prevent burning.

Serve:
- Remove toothpicks before serving. Arrange the bacon-wrapped water chestnuts on a serving platter and enjoy them as a delightful appetizer.

These Bacon-Wrapped Water Chestnuts are sweet, savory, and have a delightful crunch. They make for an excellent party or game-day snack!

Bacon-Wrapped Dates with Goat Cheese

Ingredients:

- 16 Medjool dates, pitted
- 4 ounces goat cheese
- 8 slices of bacon, cut in half
- Balsamic glaze for drizzling (optional)
- Toothpicks

Instructions:

Preheat Oven:
- Preheat your oven to 375°F (190°C).

Prepare Dates:
- Make a small slit in each date and remove the pit.

Stuff Dates:
- Stuff each date with a small amount of goat cheese. You can use a piping bag or a small spoon to fill the cavity.

Wrap with Bacon:
- Wrap each stuffed date with a half slice of bacon. Secure with toothpicks to hold the bacon in place.

Arrange on a Baking Sheet:
- Place the bacon-wrapped dates on a baking sheet lined with parchment paper or aluminum foil.

Bake:
- Bake in the preheated oven for 15-20 minutes or until the bacon is crispy, turning them halfway through for even cooking.

Broil (Optional):
- For extra crispiness, you can broil the bacon-wrapped dates for an additional 1-2 minutes. Watch closely to avoid burning.

Drizzle with Balsamic Glaze (Optional):
- If desired, drizzle the bacon-wrapped dates with balsamic glaze for a sweet and tangy finish.

Serve:
- Remove toothpicks before serving. Arrange the Bacon-Wrapped Dates with Goat Cheese on a serving platter for a delightful appetizer.

These savory-sweet bites are a perfect combination of rich goat cheese, sweet dates, and smoky bacon. Enjoy them at your next gathering or as an elegant appetizer!

Bacon and Cheddar Stuffed Mushrooms

Ingredients:

- 24 large white mushrooms, cleaned and stems removed
- 8 slices of bacon, cooked and crumbled
- 1 cup shredded cheddar cheese
- 1/2 cup breadcrumbs
- 1/4 cup grated Parmesan cheese
- 1/4 cup chopped fresh parsley
- 2 cloves garlic, minced
- 1/4 cup melted butter
- Salt and pepper to taste

Instructions:

Preheat Oven:
- Preheat your oven to 375°F (190°C).

Prepare Mushrooms:
- Clean the mushrooms and remove the stems. Place the mushroom caps on a baking sheet, cap side down.

Prepare Filling:
- In a bowl, combine the cooked and crumbled bacon, shredded cheddar cheese, breadcrumbs, Parmesan cheese, chopped parsley, minced garlic, melted butter, salt, and pepper. Mix until well combined.

Stuff Mushrooms:
- Spoon the filling mixture into each mushroom cap, pressing it down gently.

Bake:
- Bake in the preheated oven for 20-25 minutes or until the mushrooms are tender and the filling is golden brown.

Optional Broil:
- For an extra golden finish, you can broil the stuffed mushrooms for 1-2 minutes, watching closely to avoid burning.

Serve:
- Arrange the Bacon and Cheddar Stuffed Mushrooms on a serving platter. Garnish with additional chopped parsley if desired.

Serve Warm:
- Serve these delicious stuffed mushrooms warm as an appetizer or party snack.

These Bacon and Cheddar Stuffed Mushrooms are a savory and satisfying treat that's sure to be a hit at any gathering!

Bacon-Wrapped Asparagus

Ingredients:

- 1 bunch fresh asparagus spears, tough ends trimmed
- 8 slices of bacon, cut in half
- 2 tablespoons olive oil
- Salt and black pepper to taste
- 1 tablespoon balsamic glaze (optional, for drizzling)
- Lemon wedges for serving

Instructions:

Preheat Oven:
- Preheat your oven to 400°F (200°C).

Prepare Asparagus:
- Drizzle the trimmed asparagus spears with olive oil, then season with salt and black pepper. Toss to coat evenly.

Wrap with Bacon:
- Take a half-slice of bacon and wrap it around each asparagus spear, starting from the bottom and spiraling to the top. Place the bacon-wrapped asparagus on a baking sheet, seam side down.

Bake:
- Bake in the preheated oven for 15-20 minutes or until the bacon is crispy and the asparagus is tender. You can broil for an additional 1-2 minutes for extra crispiness.

Optional Balsamic Glaze:
- If desired, drizzle balsamic glaze over the bacon-wrapped asparagus for a sweet and tangy finish.

Serve:
- Transfer the Bacon-Wrapped Asparagus to a serving platter. Squeeze fresh lemon juice over the top or serve with lemon wedges on the side.

Serve Warm:
- Serve as an appetizer, side dish, or as part of a charcuterie board. Enjoy these flavorful and elegant bacon-wrapped asparagus spears!

This dish combines the smoky richness of bacon with the freshness of asparagus, creating a delightful appetizer or side that's easy to prepare and always a crowd-pleaser.

Candied Bacon Bites

Ingredients:

- 1 pound thick-cut bacon
- 1/2 cup brown sugar
- 1/4 cup maple syrup
- 1 teaspoon ground black pepper (optional for added kick)
- Pinch of cayenne pepper (optional for added heat)

Instructions:

Preheat Oven:
- Preheat your oven to 375°F (190°C). Line a baking sheet with parchment paper.

Prepare Bacon:
- Lay out the bacon slices on the prepared baking sheet, ensuring they do not overlap.

Candy Mixture:
- In a bowl, mix together the brown sugar, maple syrup, black pepper, and cayenne pepper (if using). Stir until the mixture is well combined.

Brush or Drizzle Mixture:
- Brush or drizzle the brown sugar mixture over each bacon slice, making sure to coat them evenly.

Bake:
- Bake in the preheated oven for 20-25 minutes or until the bacon is crispy and caramelized. Keep an eye on it to prevent burning.

Cool:
- Allow the candied bacon to cool on the baking sheet for a few minutes. It will continue to crisp up as it cools.

Optional: Break into Bites:
- Once cooled slightly but still pliable, you can break the candied bacon into bite-sized pieces.

Serve:
- Arrange the Candied Bacon Bites on a serving platter or enjoy them as a topping for desserts, salads, or as a sweet and savory snack.

These Candied Bacon Bites are a delightful combination of sweetness and smokiness, making them perfect for serving as an appetizer, party snack, or a unique addition to your favorite dishes.

Bacon-Wrapped Shrimp Skewers

Ingredients:

- 24 large shrimp, peeled and deveined
- 12 slices of bacon, cut in half
- 1/4 cup olive oil
- 2 tablespoons lemon juice
- 2 cloves garlic, minced
- 1 teaspoon smoked paprika
- 1/2 teaspoon black pepper
- 1/4 teaspoon cayenne pepper (optional, for heat)
- Fresh parsley, chopped, for garnish
- Lemon wedges for serving

Instructions:

Marinate Shrimp:
- In a bowl, combine olive oil, lemon juice, minced garlic, smoked paprika, black pepper, and cayenne pepper (if using). Mix well. Add the peeled and deveined shrimp to the marinade, ensuring they are well-coated. Allow them to marinate for 15-30 minutes.

Preheat Grill or Oven:
- Preheat your grill or oven to medium-high heat.

Wrap with Bacon:
- Take a half-slice of bacon and wrap it around each marinated shrimp. Thread the bacon-wrapped shrimp onto skewers, ensuring the bacon is secured.

Grill or Bake:
- Grill the bacon-wrapped shrimp skewers for 3-4 minutes per side or until the bacon is crispy and the shrimp are opaque. If using the oven, place the skewers on a baking sheet and bake for approximately 15-20 minutes at 375°F (190°C), turning halfway through.

Garnish:
- Sprinkle the cooked bacon-wrapped shrimp skewers with chopped fresh parsley.

Serve:
- Serve the Bacon-Wrapped Shrimp Skewers hot with lemon wedges on the side for squeezing over the top.

These Bacon-Wrapped Shrimp Skewers are a fantastic appetizer for parties, barbecues, or any occasion where you want to impress with a delightful combination of bacon-wrapped goodness and succulent shrimp.

Bacon and Cheese Stuffed Jalapeño

Ingredients:

- 12 large jalapeño peppers, halved lengthwise and seeds removed
- 8 ounces cream cheese, softened
- 1 cup shredded cheddar cheese
- 1/2 cup cooked and crumbled bacon
- 1/2 teaspoon garlic powder
- 1/2 teaspoon onion powder
- 1/4 teaspoon smoked paprika
- Salt and black pepper to taste
- 12 slices of bacon (for wrapping)
- Toothpicks

Instructions:

Preheat Oven:
- Preheat your oven to 375°F (190°C).

Prepare Jalapeños:
- Halve the jalapeño peppers lengthwise and remove the seeds and membranes. Wear gloves or wash hands thoroughly afterward to avoid irritation.

Prepare Filling:
- In a bowl, mix together the softened cream cheese, shredded cheddar cheese, crumbled bacon, garlic powder, onion powder, smoked paprika, salt, and black pepper until well combined.

Stuff Jalapeños:
- Spoon the cream cheese mixture into each jalapeño half, filling them evenly.

Wrap with Bacon:
- Take a slice of bacon and wrap it around each stuffed jalapeño, securing it with a toothpick.

Bake:
- Place the bacon-wrapped jalapeños on a baking sheet lined with parchment paper. Bake in the preheated oven for 20-25 minutes or until the bacon is crispy.

Broil (Optional):
- If you prefer extra crispiness, you can broil the bacon-wrapped jalapeños for an additional 1-2 minutes, watching closely to avoid burning.

Serve:
- Remove toothpicks before serving. Arrange the Bacon and Cheese Stuffed Jalapeños on a serving platter.

These Bacon and Cheese Stuffed Jalapeños are a delicious and spicy appetizer, perfect for parties or game nights. Enjoy with caution, as they can be hot!

Bacon-Wrapped Potato Bites

Ingredients:

- 24 small potatoes (baby potatoes or fingerling potatoes work well)
- 12 slices of bacon, cut in half
- 1/2 cup sour cream
- 1/4 cup chopped chives or green onions
- Salt and black pepper to taste
- Toothpicks

Instructions:

Preheat Oven:
- Preheat your oven to 400°F (200°C).

Prepare Potatoes:
- Wash and scrub the small potatoes. If they are larger, you can cut them in half.

Parboil Potatoes:
- Place the potatoes in a pot of boiling salted water for about 5-7 minutes or until they are just starting to become tender. Drain and let them cool slightly.

Wrap with Bacon:
- Take a half-slice of bacon and wrap it around each parboiled potato. Secure with toothpicks to hold the bacon in place.

Bake:
- Place the bacon-wrapped potato bites on a baking sheet lined with parchment paper. Bake in the preheated oven for 20-25 minutes or until the bacon is crispy and the potatoes are fully cooked.

Garnish:
- While the bacon-wrapped potato bites are baking, mix the sour cream with chopped chives or green onions. Season with salt and black pepper.

Serve:
- Once out of the oven, let the Bacon-Wrapped Potato Bites cool slightly. Remove toothpicks before serving. Serve them with the sour cream and chive dip on the side.

These Bacon-Wrapped Potato Bites make for a delicious appetizer or side dish, combining the savory goodness of bacon with the comforting taste of roasted potatoes. Enjoy!

Bacon-Wrapped Mozzarella Sticks

Ingredients:

- 12 mozzarella sticks, cut in half
- 12 slices of bacon, cut in half
- 1/2 cup brown sugar
- 1 teaspoon smoked paprika
- 1/2 teaspoon garlic powder
- 1/2 teaspoon onion powder
- 1/4 teaspoon black pepper
- Toothpicks

Instructions:

Preheat Oven:
- Preheat your oven to 400°F (200°C). Line a baking sheet with parchment paper.

Prepare Mozzarella Sticks:
- Cut each mozzarella stick in half to create smaller pieces.

Wrap with Bacon:
- Take a half-slice of bacon and wrap it around each mozzarella stick half. Secure with toothpicks to hold the bacon in place.

Prepare Brown Sugar Mixture:
- In a bowl, combine brown sugar, smoked paprika, garlic powder, onion powder, and black pepper. Mix well.

Coat with Brown Sugar Mixture:
- Roll each bacon-wrapped mozzarella stick in the brown sugar mixture, ensuring they are well-coated.

Bake:
- Place the bacon-wrapped mozzarella sticks on the prepared baking sheet. Bake in the preheated oven for 15-20 minutes or until the bacon is crispy and the cheese is melted.

Cool and Remove Toothpicks:
- Allow the Bacon-Wrapped Mozzarella Sticks to cool slightly before removing the toothpicks.

Serve:
- Serve these delicious appetizers as a savory and sweet treat. They can be enjoyed on their own or with your favorite dipping sauce.

These Bacon-Wrapped Mozzarella Sticks are a delightful twist on a classic snack, combining the gooey goodness of melted cheese with the savory flavor of crispy bacon. Enjoy!

Main Courses:

Bacon-Wrapped Meatloaf

Ingredients:

For the Meatloaf:

- 2 pounds ground beef (or a mixture of beef and pork)
- 1 cup breadcrumbs
- 1 cup milk
- 2 large eggs
- 1/2 cup diced onion
- 1/2 cup diced bell pepper
- 2 cloves garlic, minced
- 1/4 cup ketchup
- 2 tablespoons Worcestershire sauce
- 1 teaspoon dried thyme
- 1 teaspoon dried oregano
- Salt and black pepper to taste

For Wrapping:

- 10-12 slices of bacon

For Glaze:

- 1/2 cup ketchup
- 2 tablespoons brown sugar
- 1 tablespoon Dijon mustard

Instructions:

Preheat Oven:
- Preheat your oven to 375°F (190°C).

Prepare Meatloaf Mixture:
- In a large bowl, combine ground beef, breadcrumbs, milk, eggs, diced onion, diced bell pepper, minced garlic, ketchup, Worcestershire sauce, dried thyme, dried oregano, salt, and black pepper. Mix until well combined.

Shape Meatloaf:
- Form the meat mixture into a loaf shape on a baking sheet or in a baking dish.

Wrap with Bacon:
- Lay the bacon slices over the top of the meatloaf, tucking the ends underneath. Ensure the entire meatloaf is covered with bacon.

Prepare Glaze:
- In a small bowl, mix together ketchup, brown sugar, and Dijon mustard to create the glaze.

Brush with Glaze:
- Brush the glaze over the bacon-wrapped meatloaf, ensuring an even coating.

Bake:
- Bake in the preheated oven for 1 hour or until the internal temperature reaches 160°F (71°C).

Broil (Optional):
- If you prefer a crispier bacon, broil the meatloaf for an additional 2-3 minutes, watching closely to prevent burning.

Rest and Slice:
- Allow the Bacon-Wrapped Meatloaf to rest for a few minutes before slicing.

Serve:
- Serve the slices with your favorite sides. Enjoy this flavorful and comforting dish!

This Bacon-Wrapped Meatloaf is a delicious twist on a classic comfort food, combining the rich flavors of bacon with a well-seasoned meatloaf. Perfect for a hearty family dinner!

Bacon-Wrapped Chicken Breast

Ingredients:

- 4 boneless, skinless chicken breasts
- 8 slices of bacon
- 1 teaspoon garlic powder
- 1 teaspoon onion powder
- 1 teaspoon smoked paprika
- 1/2 teaspoon dried thyme
- Salt and black pepper to taste
- 2 tablespoons olive oil
- Fresh parsley, chopped (for garnish, optional)

Instructions:

Preheat Oven:
- Preheat your oven to 375°F (190°C).

Season Chicken:
- In a small bowl, mix together garlic powder, onion powder, smoked paprika, dried thyme, salt, and black pepper.

Season and Wrap Chicken:
- Season each chicken breast with the spice mixture. Wrap each seasoned chicken breast with 2 slices of bacon, securing the ends with toothpicks if needed.

Sear in Oven-Safe Pan (Optional):
- If you have an oven-safe pan, you can sear the bacon-wrapped chicken breasts in olive oil over medium-high heat for 2-3 minutes per side until the bacon gets a bit crispy.

Bake:
- Alternatively, place the bacon-wrapped chicken breasts on a baking sheet lined with parchment paper or in an oven-safe pan. Bake in the preheated oven for 25-30 minutes or until the chicken is cooked through and the bacon is crispy.

Broil (Optional):
- If you want the bacon extra crispy, you can broil the bacon-wrapped chicken for an additional 1-2 minutes, watching closely to prevent burning.

Rest and Garnish:

- Allow the Bacon-Wrapped Chicken Breast to rest for a few minutes before removing toothpicks (if used). Garnish with chopped fresh parsley if desired.

Serve:
- Serve the bacon-wrapped chicken breasts with your favorite sides. Enjoy this savory and flavorful dish!

These Bacon-Wrapped Chicken Breasts are a delicious and visually appealing main course. The bacon adds a smoky flavor, while keeping the chicken moist and flavorful. Perfect for a special dinner!

Bacon-Wrapped Pork Tenderloin

Ingredients:

- 1 pork tenderloin (about 1.5 to 2 pounds)
- 8-10 slices of bacon
- 2 tablespoons Dijon mustard
- 2 tablespoons maple syrup
- 1 teaspoon garlic powder
- 1 teaspoon dried thyme
- Salt and black pepper to taste
- Olive oil (for searing, optional)

Instructions:

Preheat Oven:
- Preheat your oven to 375°F (190°C).

Prepare Pork Tenderloin:
- Trim any excess fat or silver skin from the pork tenderloin. Pat it dry with paper towels.

Season and Wrap with Bacon:
- In a small bowl, mix together Dijon mustard, maple syrup, garlic powder, dried thyme, salt, and black pepper. Brush the pork tenderloin with the mustard mixture. Wrap the pork tenderloin with bacon slices, securing the ends with toothpicks if needed.

Sear (Optional):
- If desired, heat olive oil in an oven-safe skillet over medium-high heat. Sear the bacon-wrapped pork tenderloin on all sides until the bacon gets a bit crispy.

Brush with Mustard Mixture:
- Brush the bacon-wrapped pork tenderloin with more of the mustard mixture.

Bake:
- Place the bacon-wrapped pork tenderloin on a baking sheet or keep it in the skillet if it's oven-safe. Bake in the preheated oven for 25-30 minutes or until the internal temperature reaches 145°F (63°C) for medium doneness.

Broil (Optional):
- If you want the bacon extra crispy, you can broil the bacon-wrapped pork tenderloin for an additional 1-2 minutes, watching closely to prevent burning.

Rest:
- Allow the Bacon-Wrapped Pork Tenderloin to rest for 5-10 minutes before slicing.

Slice and Serve:
- Remove toothpicks (if used) and slice the bacon-wrapped pork tenderloin into medallions. Serve with any remaining mustard mixture for dipping.

This Bacon-Wrapped Pork Tenderloin is a flavorful and succulent dish with the bacon adding a smoky and savory touch. It's perfect for a special dinner or holiday meal!

Bacon-Wrapped BBQ Chicken Skewers

Ingredients:

- 2 boneless, skinless chicken breasts, cut into bite-sized chunks
- 12 slices of bacon, cut in half
- 1 cup barbecue sauce
- 1 tablespoon olive oil
- 1 teaspoon smoked paprika
- 1/2 teaspoon garlic powder
- Salt and black pepper to taste
- Wooden or metal skewers

Instructions:

Preheat Grill or Oven:
- Preheat your grill or oven to medium-high heat.

Marinate Chicken:
- In a bowl, mix together olive oil, smoked paprika, garlic powder, salt, and black pepper. Add the chicken chunks to the marinade, ensuring they are well-coated. Let them marinate for at least 15-30 minutes.

Wrap with Bacon:
- Wrap each marinated chicken chunk with a half-slice of bacon. Thread the bacon-wrapped chicken onto skewers, alternating between chicken and bacon.

Brush with BBQ Sauce:
- Brush the bacon-wrapped chicken skewers with barbecue sauce, ensuring an even coating.

Grill or Bake:
- Grill the skewers for about 15-20 minutes, turning occasionally, or until the chicken is cooked through and the bacon is crispy. If using the oven, you can bake them at 400°F (200°C) for approximately 20-25 minutes.

Broil (Optional):
- If you prefer extra crispiness, you can broil the skewers for an additional 1-2 minutes, watching closely to prevent burning.

Serve:
- Remove the Bacon-Wrapped BBQ Chicken Skewers from the grill or oven. Let them rest for a few minutes before serving.

Garnish (Optional):
- Garnish with chopped fresh parsley or green onions if desired.

Enjoy these Bacon-Wrapped BBQ Chicken Skewers as a flavorful and savory appetizer or main course. Perfect for summer grilling or any gathering!

Bacon and Mushroom Stuffed Chicken Thighs

Ingredients:

For the Chicken Thighs:

- 6 boneless, skin-on chicken thighs
- Salt and black pepper to taste
- 1 teaspoon garlic powder
- 1 teaspoon onion powder
- 1/2 teaspoon smoked paprika
- 1 tablespoon olive oil

For the Stuffing:

- 1 cup mushrooms, finely chopped
- 4 slices of bacon, cooked and crumbled
- 1/2 cup breadcrumbs
- 1/4 cup grated Parmesan cheese
- 2 cloves garlic, minced
- 1 tablespoon fresh parsley, chopped
- Salt and black pepper to taste

For the Pan Sauce:

- 1 cup chicken broth
- 2 tablespoons unsalted butter
- 1 tablespoon all-purpose flour
- Salt and black pepper to taste

Instructions:

Preheat Oven:
- Preheat your oven to 375°F (190°C).

Prepare Chicken Thighs:
- Pat the chicken thighs dry with paper towels. Season with salt, black pepper, garlic powder, onion powder, and smoked paprika.

Make Stuffing:
- In a bowl, combine chopped mushrooms, crumbled bacon, breadcrumbs, Parmesan cheese, minced garlic, chopped parsley, salt, and black pepper.

Stuff Chicken Thighs:
- Carefully lift the skin of each chicken thigh and stuff with the mushroom and bacon mixture.

Secure with Toothpicks:
- Secure the skin with toothpicks to hold the stuffing in place.

Sear Chicken Thighs:
- In an oven-safe skillet, heat olive oil over medium-high heat. Sear the chicken thighs, skin side down, until golden brown, about 3-4 minutes per side.

Bake:
- Transfer the skillet to the preheated oven and bake for 20-25 minutes or until the chicken reaches an internal temperature of 165°F (74°C).

Make Pan Sauce:
- While the chicken is baking, make the pan sauce. In a saucepan, melt butter over medium heat. Add flour and cook for 1-2 minutes, stirring constantly. Gradually whisk in chicken broth and continue to cook until the sauce thickens. Season with salt and black pepper to taste.

Serve:
- Once the chicken is done, remove toothpicks, and serve the Bacon and Mushroom Stuffed Chicken Thighs with the pan sauce drizzled over the top.

Enjoy these flavorful and juicy Bacon and Mushroom Stuffed Chicken Thighs for a delicious and comforting meal!

Bacon-Wrapped Salmon

Ingredients:

- 4 salmon fillets, skinless
- 8 slices of bacon
- 2 tablespoons maple syrup
- 2 tablespoons Dijon mustard
- 1 tablespoon soy sauce
- 1 teaspoon garlic powder
- 1 teaspoon lemon juice
- Fresh parsley, chopped (for garnish, optional)
- Lemon wedges (for serving)

Instructions:

Preheat Oven:
- Preheat your oven to 400°F (200°C).

Prepare Salmon:
- Pat the salmon fillets dry with paper towels. Season with salt and black pepper.

Wrap with Bacon:
- Wrap each salmon fillet with 2 slices of bacon, securing the ends with toothpicks if needed.

Prepare Glaze:
- In a small bowl, whisk together maple syrup, Dijon mustard, soy sauce, garlic powder, and lemon juice.

Brush with Glaze:
- Brush the bacon-wrapped salmon with the glaze, ensuring an even coating.

Sear (Optional):
- If desired, you can sear the bacon-wrapped salmon in an oven-safe skillet over medium-high heat for 2-3 minutes per side until the bacon gets a bit crispy.

Bake:
- Alternatively, place the bacon-wrapped salmon on a baking sheet lined with parchment paper. Bake in the preheated oven for 15-20 minutes or until the salmon is cooked through, and the bacon is crispy.

Broil (Optional):

- If you want the bacon extra crispy, you can broil the bacon-wrapped salmon for an additional 1-2 minutes, watching closely to prevent burning.

Garnish and Serve:
- Remove toothpicks (if used), garnish with chopped fresh parsley if desired, and serve the Bacon-Wrapped Salmon with lemon wedges on the side.

Enjoy this delicious Bacon-Wrapped Salmon as a flavorful and elegant main course, perfect for a special dinner or any occasion!

Bacon and Cheese Stuffed Burgers

Ingredients:

For the Patties:

- 2 pounds ground beef (80% lean)
- Salt and black pepper to taste

For the Filling:

- 8 slices of bacon, cooked and crumbled
- 1 cup shredded cheddar cheese
- 1/2 cup diced onions
- 2 cloves garlic, minced
- 2 tablespoons Worcestershire sauce
- Salt and black pepper to taste

For Assembly and Cooking:

- Hamburger buns
- Lettuce, tomato, and other burger toppings
- Additional cheese slices (optional)
- Ketchup, mustard, mayonnaise (optional)

Instructions:

Preheat Grill or Stovetop Griddle:
- Preheat your grill or stovetop griddle to medium-high heat.

Prepare Filling:
- In a bowl, combine crumbled bacon, shredded cheddar cheese, diced onions, minced garlic, Worcestershire sauce, salt, and black pepper. Mix well to create the stuffing.

Divide Ground Beef:
- Divide the ground beef into equal portions, creating both the top and bottom halves of the burger patties.

Create Indentation:
- Make an indentation in the center of each bottom patty, creating a well for the stuffing.

Add Filling:

- Spoon the bacon and cheese filling into the indentations on the bottom patties.

Top with Second Patty:
- Place the top patties over the filling and press the edges to seal, ensuring the stuffing is enclosed within the burgers.

Season Patties:
- Season the outside of each stuffed burger with salt and black pepper.

Grill or Cook on Griddle:
- Grill the stuffed burgers for approximately 4-6 minutes per side or until they reach your preferred level of doneness.

Melt Cheese (Optional):
- If using additional cheese slices, place them on top of the burgers during the last minute of cooking to melt.

Assemble Burgers:
- Toast the hamburger buns on the grill. Assemble the burgers with your preferred toppings, such as lettuce, tomato, ketchup, mustard, or mayonnaise.

Serve:
- Serve these delicious Bacon and Cheese Stuffed Burgers hot off the grill.

These stuffed burgers are a tasty and satisfying twist on the classic hamburger, with gooey melted cheese and savory bacon inside each bite. Enjoy!

Bacon-Wrapped BBQ Meatballs

Ingredients:

For the Meatballs:

- 1 pound ground beef
- 1/2 cup breadcrumbs
- 1/4 cup milk
- 1/4 cup grated Parmesan cheese
- 1/4 cup finely chopped onions
- 1 clove garlic, minced
- 1 teaspoon dried oregano
- 1 teaspoon dried basil
- Salt and black pepper to taste
- 1 large egg, beaten

For Wrapping:

- 1 pound bacon, slices cut in half

For BBQ Glaze:

- 1/2 cup barbecue sauce
- 2 tablespoons brown sugar
- 1 tablespoon Dijon mustard
- 1 tablespoon apple cider vinegar

Toothpicks for securing

Instructions:

Preheat Oven:
- Preheat your oven to 375°F (190°C).

Prepare Meatball Mixture:
- In a large bowl, combine ground beef, breadcrumbs, milk, Parmesan cheese, chopped onions, minced garlic, dried oregano, dried basil, salt, black pepper, and beaten egg. Mix until well combined.

Shape Meatballs:
- Shape the mixture into small meatballs, about 1 inch in diameter.

Wrap with Bacon:
- Wrap each meatball with a half-slice of bacon and secure with a toothpick.

Bake:
- Place the bacon-wrapped meatballs on a baking sheet lined with parchment paper. Bake in the preheated oven for 20-25 minutes or until the bacon is crispy and the meatballs are cooked through.

Prepare BBQ Glaze:
- In a small saucepan, combine barbecue sauce, brown sugar, Dijon mustard, and apple cider vinegar. Heat over medium heat, stirring, until the brown sugar is dissolved and the glaze is well combined.

Brush with Glaze:
- Brush the cooked bacon-wrapped meatballs with the BBQ glaze, ensuring they are well coated.

Broil (Optional):
- If you prefer a caramelized finish, you can broil the meatballs for an additional 1-2 minutes, watching closely to prevent burning.

Serve:
- Remove toothpicks and arrange the Bacon-Wrapped BBQ Meatballs on a serving platter. Serve with extra BBQ glaze on the side for dipping.

These Bacon-Wrapped BBQ Meatballs make for a savory and irresistible appetizer, perfect for parties or game day gatherings. Enjoy!

Bacon-Wrapped Filet Mignon

Ingredients:

- 4 filet mignon steaks, about 6 ounces each
- 8 slices of bacon
- Salt and black pepper to taste
- 2 tablespoons olive oil
- 2 cloves garlic, minced
- 2 sprigs fresh rosemary (optional)
- Butter (optional, for basting)

Instructions:

Preheat Oven:
- Preheat your oven to 400°F (200°C).

Season Filet Mignon:
- Pat the filet mignon steaks dry with paper towels. Season with salt and black pepper to taste.

Wrap with Bacon:
- Wrap each filet mignon steak with 2 slices of bacon, securing the bacon ends with toothpicks if needed.

Sear in Oven-Safe Pan:
- In an oven-safe skillet, heat olive oil over medium-high heat. Add minced garlic and optional rosemary sprigs. Sear the bacon-wrapped filet mignon steaks for 2-3 minutes per side until the bacon gets a bit crispy.

Baste with Butter (Optional):
- If desired, add a pat of butter to the pan and baste the filet mignon steaks with the melted butter for extra richness and flavor.

Finish in the Oven:
- Transfer the skillet to the preheated oven. Bake for about 10-15 minutes or until the filet mignon reaches your preferred level of doneness (medium-rare, medium, etc.).

Broil (Optional):
- If you prefer a crispier bacon, you can broil the bacon-wrapped filet mignon for an additional 1-2 minutes, watching closely to prevent burning.

Rest:
- Remove toothpicks and let the bacon-wrapped filet mignon rest for 5 minutes before serving.

Serve:
- Serve the Bacon-Wrapped Filet Mignon on a plate, and enjoy this luxurious and flavorful steak!

This Bacon-Wrapped Filet Mignon is a deliciously indulgent dish, perfect for special occasions or when you want to treat yourself to a gourmet meal at home.

Bacon-Wrapped BBQ Shrimp

Ingredients:

- 1 pound large shrimp, peeled and deveined
- 8 slices of bacon, cut in half
- 1/2 cup barbecue sauce
- 1 tablespoon honey or maple syrup
- 1 tablespoon olive oil
- 1 teaspoon smoked paprika
- 1/2 teaspoon garlic powder
- 1/2 teaspoon onion powder
- Salt and black pepper to taste
- Wooden or metal skewers

Instructions:

Preheat Grill or Oven:
- Preheat your grill or oven to medium-high heat.

Marinate Shrimp:
- In a bowl, mix together barbecue sauce, honey or maple syrup, olive oil, smoked paprika, garlic powder, onion powder, salt, and black pepper. Add the peeled and deveined shrimp to the marinade, ensuring they are well-coated. Let them marinate for at least 15-30 minutes.

Wrap with Bacon:
- Wrap each marinated shrimp with a half-slice of bacon. Thread the bacon-wrapped shrimp onto skewers, ensuring they are secured.

Brush with Marinade:
- Brush the bacon-wrapped shrimp with extra marinade for added flavor.

Grill or Bake:
- Grill the skewers for approximately 3-4 minutes per side or until the bacon is crispy, and the shrimp are cooked through. If using the oven, you can bake them at 400°F (200°C) for approximately 15-20 minutes, turning halfway through.

Broil (Optional):
- If you want the bacon extra crispy, you can broil the bacon-wrapped shrimp for an additional 1-2 minutes, watching closely to prevent burning.

Serve:
- Remove the Bacon-Wrapped BBQ Shrimp from the grill or oven. Serve them hot as an appetizer or main dish.

These Bacon-Wrapped BBQ Shrimp are a delicious combination of sweet and savory flavors, making them a perfect appetizer for parties or a tasty addition to your summer grilling menu. Enjoy!

Salads and Sides:

Bacon and Blue Cheese Wedge Salad

Ingredients:

For the Salad:

- 1 head of iceberg lettuce, cut into wedges
- 8 slices of bacon, cooked and crumbled
- 1 cup cherry tomatoes, halved
- 1/2 red onion, thinly sliced
- 1/2 cup blue cheese crumbles
- Chives, chopped (for garnish)

For the Blue Cheese Dressing:

- 1/2 cup mayonnaise
- 1/4 cup sour cream
- 1/4 cup buttermilk
- 1/2 cup blue cheese crumbles
- 1 tablespoon white wine vinegar
- 1 teaspoon Dijon mustard
- Salt and black pepper to taste

Instructions:

    Prepare Blue Cheese Dressing:
- In a bowl, whisk together mayonnaise, sour cream, buttermilk, blue cheese crumbles, white wine vinegar, Dijon mustard, salt, and black pepper. Adjust the seasoning to taste. Refrigerate the dressing until ready to use.

    Assemble Wedge Salad:
- Place the iceberg lettuce wedges on serving plates.

Top with Ingredients:
- Sprinkle crumbled bacon, cherry tomato halves, red onion slices, and blue cheese crumbles over each wedge.

Drizzle with Dressing:
- Drizzle the prepared blue cheese dressing over each wedge salad.

Garnish:
- Garnish with chopped chives for a burst of freshness.

Serve:
- Serve the Bacon and Blue Cheese Wedge Salad immediately, and enjoy the delicious combination of flavors and textures.

This Bacon and Blue Cheese Wedge Salad is a classic and satisfying dish, perfect for a refreshing and indulgent starter or side. The creamy blue cheese dressing complements the crisp bacon and fresh vegetables for a delightful taste experience.

Bacon and Brussels Sprouts Salad

Ingredients:

For the Salad:

- 1 pound Brussels sprouts, trimmed and thinly sliced
- 8 slices of bacon, cooked and crumbled
- 1/2 cup dried cranberries
- 1/4 cup chopped pecans, toasted
- 1/4 cup grated Parmesan cheese

For the Dressing:

- 3 tablespoons olive oil
- 2 tablespoons apple cider vinegar
- 1 tablespoon Dijon mustard
- 1 tablespoon honey
- Salt and black pepper to taste

Instructions:

Prepare Brussels Sprouts:
- Trim the ends of the Brussels sprouts and thinly slice them. You can also use a mandoline for a finer shred.

Cook Bacon:
- Cook the bacon until crispy, then crumble it into smaller pieces.

Toast Pecans:
- In a dry skillet over medium heat, toast the chopped pecans until they become fragrant and slightly browned. Be sure to stir frequently to avoid burning.

Assemble Salad:
- In a large salad bowl, combine the sliced Brussels sprouts, crumbled bacon, dried cranberries, toasted pecans, and grated Parmesan cheese.

Prepare Dressing:
- In a small bowl, whisk together olive oil, apple cider vinegar, Dijon mustard, honey, salt, and black pepper until well combined.

Dress the Salad:
- Pour the dressing over the salad and toss everything together until the ingredients are evenly coated.

Chill (Optional):
- If you prefer a chilled salad, refrigerate for 15-30 minutes before serving.

Serve:
- Serve the Bacon and Brussels Sprouts Salad as a flavorful and hearty side dish. Enjoy the delightful combination of crispy bacon, sweet cranberries, and the crunch of Brussels sprouts!

This salad is not only delicious but also a great way to enjoy the flavors of Brussels sprouts in a fresh and satisfying way. Perfect for a side dish or a light lunch!

Loaded Baked Potato Salad with Bacon

Ingredients:

For the Potato Salad:

- 2 pounds russet potatoes, peeled and diced
- 8 slices of bacon, cooked and crumbled
- 1 cup shredded cheddar cheese
- 1/2 cup sour cream
- 1/4 cup mayonnaise
- 1/4 cup chopped green onions
- Salt and black pepper to taste

For Topping:

- Additional shredded cheddar cheese
- Chopped green onions
- Crumbled bacon

Instructions:

Boil Potatoes:
- Place diced potatoes in a large pot of salted water. Bring to a boil and cook until potatoes are fork-tender. Drain and let them cool.

Prepare Dressing:
- In a bowl, mix together sour cream, mayonnaise, chopped green onions, salt, and black pepper to create the dressing.

Assemble Potato Salad:
- In a large mixing bowl, combine the cooled diced potatoes, crumbled bacon, shredded cheddar cheese, and the prepared dressing. Gently toss until well coated.

Chill (Optional):
- For enhanced flavor, refrigerate the Loaded Baked Potato Salad for at least 1 hour before serving.

Top and Garnish:
- Just before serving, top the potato salad with additional shredded cheddar cheese, chopped green onions, and crumbled bacon.

Serve:
- Serve the Loaded Baked Potato Salad as a delicious and satisfying side dish, perfect for picnics, barbecues, or any gathering.

This Loaded Baked Potato Salad with Bacon is a flavorful twist on a classic side dish. The combination of creamy dressing, crispy bacon, and cheesy goodness makes it a crowd-pleaser. Enjoy!

Bacon-Wrapped Asparagus Bundles

Ingredients:

- 1 pound fresh asparagus spears, trimmed
- 8-10 slices of bacon
- 2 tablespoons olive oil
- 2 tablespoons balsamic vinegar
- 1 tablespoon honey
- Salt and black pepper to taste
- Toothpicks

Instructions:

Preheat Oven:
- Preheat your oven to 400°F (200°C).

Prepare Asparagus:
- Trim the tough ends of the asparagus spears.

Wrap with Bacon:
- Divide the asparagus into bundles, typically 3-4 spears per bundle. Wrap each bundle with a slice of bacon and secure the ends with toothpicks.

Place on Baking Sheet:
- Place the bacon-wrapped asparagus bundles on a baking sheet lined with parchment paper.

Drizzle with Olive Oil:
- Drizzle olive oil over the bundles to ensure they don't stick to the pan and to add extra flavor.

Season:
- Sprinkle salt and black pepper over the bundles, to taste.

Bake:
- Bake in the preheated oven for 20-25 minutes or until the bacon is crispy and the asparagus is tender.

Prepare Glaze:
- In a small bowl, mix together balsamic vinegar and honey to create a glaze.

Brush with Glaze:
- During the last 5 minutes of baking, brush the bacon-wrapped asparagus bundles with the balsamic glaze.

Broil (Optional):

- If you prefer a caramelized finish, you can broil the bundles for an additional 1-2 minutes, watching closely to prevent burning.

Serve:
- Remove the toothpicks before serving. Arrange the Bacon-Wrapped Asparagus Bundles on a serving platter and enjoy!

These Bacon-Wrapped Asparagus Bundles make for a delightful appetizer or side dish. The smoky flavor of bacon complements the crisp-tender asparagus, creating a perfect combination. Great for entertaining or as a tasty addition to your weeknight dinner!

Bacon and Corn Salad

Ingredients:

- 4 cups fresh or frozen corn kernels (thawed if using frozen)
- 8 slices of bacon, cooked and crumbled
- 1 cup cherry tomatoes, halved
- 1/2 cup red onion, finely chopped
- 1/4 cup fresh cilantro, chopped
- 1 jalapeño, seeds removed and finely chopped (optional, for a spicy kick)

For the Dressing:

- 3 tablespoons olive oil
- 2 tablespoons lime juice
- 1 tablespoon honey
- 1 clove garlic, minced
- Salt and black pepper to taste

Instructions:

Cook Bacon:
- Cook the bacon until crispy, then crumble it into smaller pieces.

Prepare Corn:
- If using fresh corn, cook it by boiling or grilling until tender. If using frozen corn, thaw it according to package instructions.

Assemble Salad:
- In a large bowl, combine the corn, crumbled bacon, cherry tomatoes, red onion, cilantro, and jalapeño (if using).

Prepare Dressing:
- In a small bowl, whisk together olive oil, lime juice, honey, minced garlic, salt, and black pepper.

Toss with Dressing:
- Pour the dressing over the salad and toss gently until all ingredients are well coated.

Chill (Optional):
- For enhanced flavor, refrigerate the Bacon and Corn Salad for at least 30 minutes before serving.

Serve:
- Serve the salad as a refreshing side dish, perfect for barbecues, picnics, or any occasion.

This Bacon and Corn Salad is a delicious blend of sweet and savory flavors with a hint of freshness from the lime and cilantro. It's a versatile dish that pairs well with grilled meats or as a standalone salad. Enjoy!

Creamy Bacon Coleslaw

Ingredients:

For the Coleslaw:

- 1 medium head of green cabbage, finely shredded
- 2 medium carrots, grated
- 1/2 cup red onion, thinly sliced
- 8 slices of bacon, cooked and crumbled
- 1/4 cup fresh parsley, chopped (optional, for garnish)

For the Dressing:

- 1 cup mayonnaise
- 1/4 cup sour cream
- 2 tablespoons apple cider vinegar
- 1 tablespoon Dijon mustard
- 1 tablespoon honey
- Salt and black pepper to taste

Instructions:

Prepare Coleslaw Vegetables:
- Finely shred the green cabbage, grate the carrots, and thinly slice the red onion. Place them in a large bowl.

Cook Bacon:
- Cook the bacon until crispy, then crumble it into smaller pieces.

Assemble Coleslaw:
- Add the crumbled bacon to the bowl with shredded vegetables. Toss to combine.

Prepare Dressing:
- In a separate bowl, whisk together mayonnaise, sour cream, apple cider vinegar, Dijon mustard, honey, salt, and black pepper. Adjust the seasoning to taste.

Combine Dressing with Coleslaw:
- Pour the dressing over the coleslaw mixture. Toss until all the ingredients are well coated with the creamy dressing.

Chill (Optional):
- Refrigerate the Creamy Bacon Coleslaw for at least 30 minutes before serving for enhanced flavor.

Garnish and Serve:

- Garnish with chopped fresh parsley before serving. Serve as a side dish at barbecues, picnics, or alongside your favorite grilled meats.

This Creamy Bacon Coleslaw is a delightful twist on classic coleslaw, adding a smoky and savory flavor with the addition of crispy bacon. It's a crowd-pleaser and a great complement to a variety of dishes!

Bacon and Cheese Loaded Sweet Potatoes

Ingredients:

- 4 medium-sized sweet potatoes
- 8 slices of bacon, cooked and crumbled
- 1 cup shredded cheddar cheese
- 1/2 cup sour cream
- 2 green onions, thinly sliced
- Salt and black pepper to taste
- Fresh parsley, chopped (optional, for garnish)

Instructions:

Preheat Oven:
- Preheat your oven to 400°F (200°C).

Bake Sweet Potatoes:
- Wash and scrub the sweet potatoes. Pierce each sweet potato several times with a fork. Place them on a baking sheet and bake in the preheated oven for about 45-60 minutes or until they are fork-tender.

Cool and Slice:
- Allow the baked sweet potatoes to cool slightly. Cut a slit lengthwise in the center of each sweet potato, creating a pocket for the filling.

Fluff and Season:
- Gently fluff the insides of the sweet potatoes with a fork. Season with salt and black pepper to taste.

Fill with Goodies:
- Divide the crumbled bacon and shredded cheddar cheese evenly among the sweet potatoes, stuffing the filling into the pockets.

Bake Again:
- Place the stuffed sweet potatoes back in the oven for about 5-10 minutes or until the cheese is melted and bubbly.

Top with Sour Cream and Green Onions:
- Remove the sweet potatoes from the oven. Top each one with a dollop of sour cream and sprinkle sliced green onions on top.

Garnish (Optional):
- Garnish with chopped fresh parsley if desired.

Serve:
- Serve the Bacon and Cheese Loaded Sweet Potatoes hot as a delicious and comforting side dish.

This recipe turns sweet potatoes into a savory delight with the addition of bacon and cheese. It's a perfect side dish for any occasion, and the combination of flavors will leave you craving more!

Bacon and Ranch Pasta Salad

Ingredients:

For the Pasta Salad:

- 8 ounces rotini or your favorite pasta, cooked and drained
- 8 slices of bacon, cooked and crumbled
- 1 cup cherry tomatoes, halved
- 1 cup broccoli florets, blanched
- 1/2 cup red bell pepper, diced
- 1/2 cup black olives, sliced
- 1/2 cup cheddar cheese, cubed

For the Ranch Dressing:

- 1 cup mayonnaise
- 1/2 cup sour cream
- 1 tablespoon ranch seasoning mix
- 1 tablespoon apple cider vinegar
- 1 tablespoon fresh chives, chopped
- Salt and black pepper to taste

Instructions:

Cook Pasta:
- Cook the pasta according to the package instructions. Drain and let it cool.

Prepare Vegetables:
- Blanch the broccoli florets in boiling water for 1-2 minutes, then transfer to ice water to stop the cooking process. Slice the cherry tomatoes, dice the red bell pepper, and slice the black olives.

Prepare Bacon:
- Cook the bacon until crispy, then crumble it into smaller pieces.

Assemble Pasta Salad:
- In a large bowl, combine the cooked and cooled pasta, crumbled bacon, cherry tomatoes, blanched broccoli, diced red bell pepper, sliced black olives, and cubed cheddar cheese.

Prepare Ranch Dressing:

- In a separate bowl, whisk together mayonnaise, sour cream, ranch seasoning mix, apple cider vinegar, chopped chives, salt, and black pepper. Adjust the seasoning to taste.

Toss with Dressing:
- Pour the ranch dressing over the pasta salad and toss until all ingredients are well coated.

Chill (Optional):
- Refrigerate the Bacon and Ranch Pasta Salad for at least 1 hour before serving for enhanced flavor.

Serve:
- Serve the pasta salad as a refreshing side dish for picnics, barbecues, or any gathering.

This Bacon and Ranch Pasta Salad combines the smoky goodness of bacon with the zesty flavors of ranch dressing, creating a delicious and satisfying dish that everyone will enjoy.

Bacon and Garlic Green Beans

Ingredients:

- 1 pound fresh green beans, trimmed
- 8 slices of bacon, diced
- 4 cloves garlic, minced
- 2 tablespoons olive oil
- Salt and black pepper to taste
- Red pepper flakes (optional, for heat)
- 1 tablespoon fresh lemon juice (optional, for brightness)
- Fresh parsley, chopped (for garnish)

Instructions:

Blanch Green Beans:
- Bring a large pot of salted water to a boil. Add the green beans and cook for 2-3 minutes until they are bright green and slightly tender. Immediately transfer them to an ice water bath to stop the cooking process. Drain and set aside.

Cook Bacon:
- In a large skillet over medium heat, cook the diced bacon until it becomes crispy. Remove bacon from the pan and place it on a paper towel-lined plate to drain excess grease.

Sauté Garlic:
- In the same skillet, add olive oil and minced garlic. Sauté for about 30 seconds to 1 minute until the garlic becomes fragrant.

Add Green Beans:
- Add the blanched green beans to the skillet with garlic. Toss to coat the beans in the garlic-infused oil.

Mix in Bacon:
- Add the cooked bacon to the skillet with green beans. Toss everything together until well combined.

Season and Spice:
- Season with salt and black pepper to taste. If you like a bit of heat, you can add red pepper flakes. Squeeze fresh lemon juice over the green beans for a burst of brightness.

Sauté Until Crisp-Tender:
- Continue to sauté the green beans for an additional 2-3 minutes or until they reach your desired level of crisp-tenderness.

Garnish and Serve:
- Garnish the Bacon and Garlic Green Beans with chopped fresh parsley. Serve hot as a flavorful side dish.

This Bacon and Garlic Green Beans recipe adds a savory and smoky twist to the classic green bean side dish. The combination of bacon and garlic enhances the natural flavors of the green beans, creating a delicious and satisfying side for any meal. Enjoy!

Bacon and Potato Casserole

Ingredients:

- 4 cups potatoes, peeled and thinly sliced
- 8 slices of bacon, cooked and crumbled
- 1 cup shredded cheddar cheese
- 1/2 cup diced onions
- 2 cloves garlic, minced
- 1 cup sour cream
- 1/2 cup mayonnaise
- 1 teaspoon dried thyme
- Salt and black pepper to taste
- Chives, chopped (for garnish)

Instructions:

Preheat Oven:
- Preheat your oven to 350°F (175°C).

Prepare Potatoes:
- Peel and thinly slice the potatoes. Parboil the potato slices in boiling water for 5 minutes to slightly soften them. Drain and set aside.

Cook Bacon:
- Cook the bacon until crispy, then crumble it into smaller pieces.

Prepare Casserole Dish:
- Grease a baking dish with butter or cooking spray.

Layer Potatoes and Bacon:
- In the prepared baking dish, layer half of the parboiled potato slices. Sprinkle half of the crumbled bacon, diced onions, minced garlic, and shredded cheddar cheese over the potatoes. Repeat with the remaining potatoes, bacon, onions, garlic, and cheese.

Prepare Creamy Mixture:
- In a bowl, mix together sour cream, mayonnaise, dried thyme, salt, and black pepper.

Pour Creamy Mixture:
- Pour the sour cream mixture evenly over the layered potatoes and bacon in the baking dish.

Bake:
- Bake in the preheated oven for 40-45 minutes or until the potatoes are tender, and the top is golden brown.

Garnish:

- Garnish the Bacon and Potato Casserole with chopped chives.

Serve:
- Allow the casserole to cool for a few minutes before serving. Serve as a hearty side dish for any meal.

This Bacon and Potato Casserole is a comforting and flavorful dish that combines the richness of bacon and the creaminess of sour cream for a satisfying experience. Perfect for gatherings or as a comforting family dinner side dish!